S O C I A L
introduction

nO MATTER WHAT STAGE YOUR SOCIAL ANIMAL IS AT – CATERPILLAR, COCOON OR BUTTERFLY – YOU MUST STAY ON TOP OF IT ALL. KEEP TRACK, KEEP NOTE, KEEP IT STRAIGHT. ALL YOUR NEWS THAT'S FIT TO PRINT. PUT FRIENDS IN THEIR PROPER PLACES. PUT PLACES IN THE PROPER PERSPECTIVE. RATE IT, GRADE IT, RANT IT AND RAVE IT. LIST THIS AND THAT AND THE OTHER. AUTHOR YOUR VERY OWN SOCIAL STUDIES REFERENCE WORK (OF COURSE, YOURS WILL BE COOL).

Socialites

one

LOYAL
FRIEND
IS WORTH
TEN THOUSAND
RELATIVES.

Socialites

- NAME:

- NICKNAME:

- BIRTHDAY:

- ADDRESS:

- PHONE:

- EMAIL:

- STUFF THEY LIKE:

- STUFF THEY HATE:

- STUFF THEY DO:

Socialites

- **NAME:**

- **NICKNAME:**

- **BIRTHDAY:**

- **ADDRESS:**

- **PHONE:**

- **EMAIL:**

- **STUFF THEY LIKE:**

- **STUFF THEY HATE:**

- **STUFF THEY DO:**

Socialites

- NAME:

- NICKNAME:

- BIRTHDAY:

- ADDRESS:

- PHONE:

- EMAIL:

- STUFF THEY LIKE:

- STUFF THEY HATE:

- STUFF THEY DO:

Socialites

- NAME:

- NICKNAME:

- BIRTHDAY:

- ADDRESS:

- PHONE:

- EMAIL:

- STUFF THEY LIKE:

- STUFF THEY HATE:

- STUFF THEY DO:

Socialites

- NAME:

- NICKNAME:

- BIRTHDAY:

- ADDRESS:

- PHONE:

- EMAIL:

- STUFF THEY LIKE:

- STUFF THEY HATE:

- STUFF THEY DO:

Socialites

- NAME:

- NICKNAME:

- BIRTHDAY:

- ADDRESS:

- PHONE:

- EMAIL:

- STUFF THEY LIKE:

- STUFF THEY HATE:

- STUFF THEY DO:

friendship
is a *plant*

we must
often
water.

Socialites

- **NAME:**

- **NICKNAME:**

- **BIRTHDAY:**

- **ADDRESS:**

- **PHONE:**

- **EMAIL:**

- **STUFF THEY LIKE:**

- **STUFF THEY HATE:**

- **STUFF THEY DO:**

Socialites

- **NAME:**

- **NICKNAME:**

- **BIRTHDAY:**

- **ADDRESS:**

- **PHONE:**

- **EMAIL:**

- **STUFF THEY LIKE:**

- **STUFF THEY HATE:**

- **STUFF THEY DO:**

Socialites

🌙 **NAME:**

🌙 **NICKNAME:**

🌙 **BIRTHDAY:**

🌙 **ADDRESS:**

🌙 **PHONE:**

🌙 **EMAIL:**

🌙 **STUFF THEY LIKE:**

🌙 **STUFF THEY HATE:**

🌙 **STUFF THEY DO:**

Socialites

- NAME:

- NICKNAME:

- BIRTHDAY:

- ADDRESS:

- PHONE:

- EMAIL:

- STUFF THEY LIKE:

- STUFF THEY HATE:

- STUFF THEY DO:

Socialites

🦢 **NAME:**

🦢 **NICKNAME:**

🦢 **BIRTHDAY:**

🦢 **ADDRESS:**

🦢 **PHONE:**

🦢 **EMAIL:**

🦢 **STUFF THEY LIKE:**

🦢 **STUFF THEY HATE:**

🦢 **STUFF THEY DO:**

Socialites

- **NAME:**

- **NICKNAME:**

- **BIRTHDAY:**

- **ADDRESS:**

- **PHONE:**

- **EMAIL:**

- **STUFF THEY LIKE:**

- **STUFF THEY HATE:**

- **STUFF THEY DO:**

friends

are lost

by calling

often

and

calling

seldom.

Socialites

- NAME:

- NICKNAME:

- BIRTHDAY:

- ADDRESS:

- PHONE:

- EMAIL:

- STUFF THEY LIKE:

- STUFF THEY HATE:

- STUFF THEY DO:

Socialites

- NAME:

- NICKNAME:

- BIRTHDAY:

- ADDRESS:

- PHONE:

- EMAIL:

- STUFF THEY LIKE:

- STUFF THEY HATE:

- STUFF THEY DO:

Socialites

- NAME:

- NICKNAME:

- BIRTHDAY:

- ADDRESS:

- PHONE:

- EMAIL:

- STUFF THEY LIKE:

- STUFF THEY HATE:

- STUFF THEY DO:

Socialites

- **NAME:**

- **NICKNAME:**

- **BIRTHDAY:**

- **ADDRESS:**

- **PHONE:**

- **EMAIL:**

- **STUFF THEY LIKE:**

- **STUFF THEY HATE:**

- **STUFF THEY DO:**

Socialites

- **NAME:**

- **NICKNAME:**

- **BIRTHDAY:**

- **ADDRESS:**

- **PHONE:**

- **EMAIL:**

- **STUFF THEY LIKE:**

- **STUFF THEY HATE:**

- **STUFF THEY DO:**

Socialites

- NAME:

- NICKNAME:

- BIRTHDAY:

- ADDRESS:

- PHONE:

- EMAIL:

- STUFF THEY LIKE:

- STUFF THEY HATE:

- STUFF THEY DO:

A FRIEND

IS SOMEONE

WHO KNOWS

ALL ABOUT YOU,

AND

STILL

LIKES

YOU.

Socialites

- **NAME:**

- **NICKNAME:**

- **BIRTHDAY:**

- **ADDRESS:**

- **PHONE:**

- **EMAIL:**

- **STUFF THEY LIKE:**

- **STUFF THEY HATE:**

- **STUFF THEY DO:**

Socialites

🍃 **NAME:**

🍃 **NICKNAME:**

🍃 **BIRTHDAY:**

🍃 **ADDRESS:**

🍃 **PHONE:**

🍃 **EMAIL:**

🍃 **STUFF THEY LIKE:**

🍃 **STUFF THEY HATE:**

🍃 **STUFF THEY DO:**

Socialites

🐾 **NAME:**

🐾 **NICKNAME:**

🐾 **BIRTHDAY:**

🐾 **ADDRESS:**

🐾 **PHONE:**

🐾 **EMAIL:**

🐾 **STUFF THEY LIKE:**

🐾 **STUFF THEY HATE:**

🐾 **STUFF THEY DO:**

Socialites

🐾 **NAME:**

🐾 **NICKNAME:**

🐾 **BIRTHDAY:**

🐾 **ADDRESS:**

🐾 **PHONE:**

🐾 **EMAIL:**

🐾 **STUFF THEY LIKE:**

🐾 **STUFF THEY HATE:**

🐾 **STUFF THEY DO:**

Socialites

🐾 **NAME:**

🐾 **NICKNAME:**

🐾 **BIRTHDAY:**

🐾 **ADDRESS:**

🐾 **PHONE:**

🐾 **EMAIL:**

🐾 **STUFF THEY LIKE:**

🐾 **STUFF THEY HATE:**

🐾 **STUFF THEY DO:**

Socialites

- **NAME:**

- **NICKNAME:**

- **BIRTHDAY:**

- **ADDRESS:**

- **PHONE:**

- **EMAIL:**

- **STUFF THEY LIKE:**

- **STUFF THEY HATE:**

- **STUFF THEY DO:**

Socialites

🐾 **NAME:**

🐾 **NICKNAME:**

🐾 **BIRTHDAY:**

🐾 **ADDRESS:**

🐾 **PHONE:**

🐾 **EMAIL:**

🐾 **STUFF THEY LIKE:**

🐾 **STUFF THEY HATE:**

🐾 **STUFF THEY DO:**

Socialites

- NAME:

- NICKNAME:

- BIRTHDAY:

- ADDRESS:

- PHONE:

- EMAIL:

- STUFF THEY LIKE:

- STUFF THEY HATE:

- STUFF THEY DO:

A PLACE
FOR
EVERYTHING
AND

SUPER SPOTS

HOT SPOT

BEST OF

WORST OF

SUPER SPOTS

HOT SPOT

BEST OF

WORST OF

HOT SPOT

BEST OF

WORST OF

SUPER SPOTS

HOT SPOT

BEST OF

WORST OF

YOU GO...THERE YOU ARE... YOU ARE...WHEREVER YOU GO...THERE YOU ARE. WHEREVER YOU GO...THERE YOU ARE...WHEREVER YOU GO...THERE YOU ARE...WHEREVER

SUPER SPOTS

HOT SPOT

BEST OF

WORST OF

SUPER SPOTS

HOT SPOT

BEST OF

WORST OF

SUPER SPOTS

HOT SPOT

BEST OF

WORST OF

SUPER SPOTS

HOT SPOT

BEST OF

WORST OF

ONE
CANNOT BE IN
TWO
PLACES AT
ONCE . . .

SO ENJOY WHEREVER YOU ARE.

Scandalous Speeches

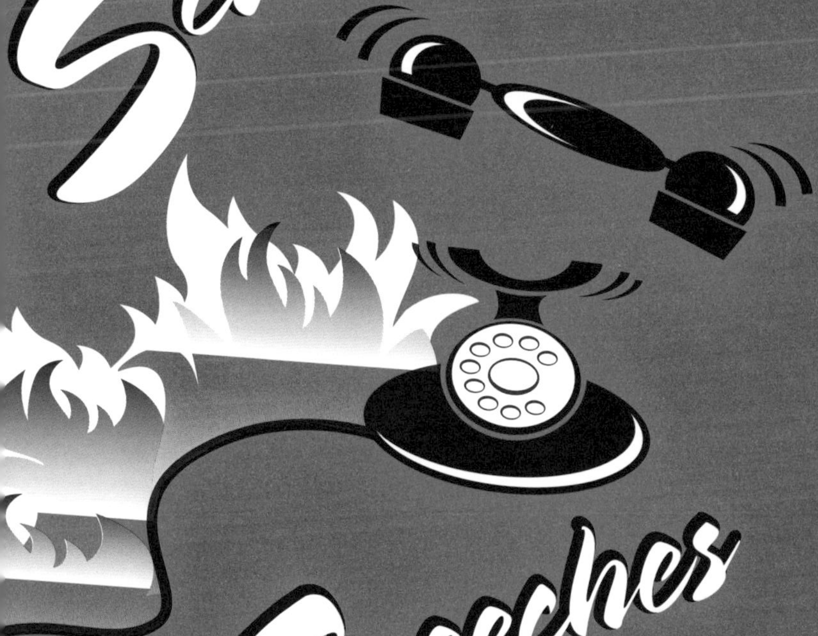

Whoever gossips to you,

will gossip
of you.

Scandalous Speeches

 HE SAID:

 SHE SAID:

 **THE BUZZ:**

 **OLD NEWS:**

 MY TAKE:

Scandalous Speeches

 HE SAID:

 SHE SAID:

THE BUZZ:

OLD NEWS:

MY TAKE:

Scandalous Speeches

 HE SAID:

 **SHE SAID:**

THE BUZZ:

 OLD NEWS:

MY TAKE:

Scandalous Speeches

 HE SAID:

 SHE SAID:

 **THE BUZZ:**

 OLD NEWS:

 MY TAKE:

IT IS BETTER
TO CONCEAL
ONE'S KNOWLEDGE

THAN TO
REVEAL ONE'S
IGNORANCE.

Scandalous Speeches

🔥 **HE SAID:**

🔥 **SHE SAID:**

〰️ **THE BUZZ:**

📢 **OLD NEWS:**

 MY TAKE:

Scandalous Speeches

 HE SAID:

 SHE SAID:

 **THE BUZZ:**

 OLD NEWS:

 MY TAKE:

Scandalous Speeches

 HE SAID:

 SHE SAID:

 **THE BUZZ:**

 **OLD NEWS:**

 MY TAKE:

Scandalous Speeches

 HE SAID:

 SHE SAID:

〜〜〜 **THE BUZZ:**

〜〜 **OLD NEWS:**

▦ **MY TAKE:**

a TONGUE
   CAN BREAK
a NOSE.

Scandalous Speeches

 HE SAID:

SHE SAID:

THE BUZZ:

OLD NEWS:

 MY TAKE:

Scandalous Speeches

 HE SAID:

 SHE SAID:

 **THE BUZZ:**

 **OLD NEWS:**

 MY TAKE:

Scandalous Speeches

 HE SAID:

 SHE SAID:

 **THE BUZZ:**

 OLD NEWS:

 MY TAKE:

Scandalous Speeches

 HE SAID:

SHE SAID:

 THE BUZZ:

OLD NEWS:

MY TAKE:

WAS NEVER WRITTEN DOWN.

Scandalous Speeches

 HE SAID:

SHE SAID:

THE BUZZ:

OLD NEWS:

MY TAKE:

Scandalous Speeches

 HE SAID:

 SHE SAID:

 **THE BUZZ:**

 OLD NEWS:

 MY TAKE:

Scandalous Speeches

 HE SAID:

 SHE SAID:

 **THE BUZZ:**

 **OLD NEWS:**

 MY TAKE:

Scandalous Speeches

 HE SAID:

 SHE SAID:

 **THE BUZZ:**

 OLD NEWS:

 MY TAKE:

TOP SHOPS

Don't be a
slave to style
or a victim
of fashion.

SHOPPING BUDS

GOTTA HAVES

GOTTA HAVES

SUBSTANTIAL

STYLE

FOLLOWS

SECURE SUBSTANCE

a *celebrity* is

someone who

works a lifetime

for **fame**

and then wears

sunglasses to

avoid being

recognized.

NAME:

BORN:

LIVES:

MY FAVORITE WORKS:

HIS/HER FAVORITE STUFF:

DATES:

HANGS WITH:

OTHER:

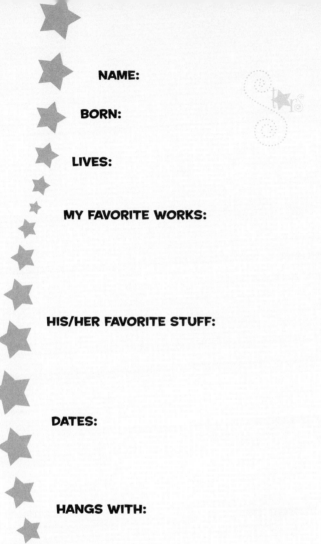

NAME:

BORN:

LIVES:

MY FAVORITE WORKS:

HIS/HER FAVORITE STUFF:

DATES:

HANGS WITH:

OTHER:

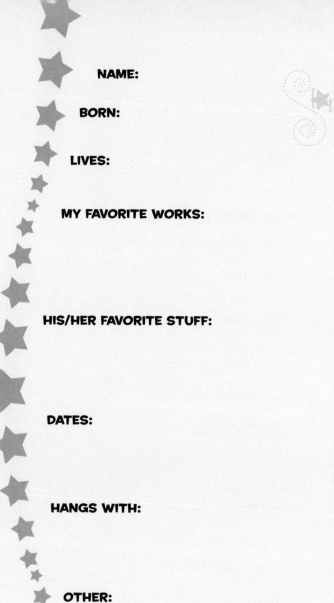

NAME:

BORN:

LIVES:

MY FAVORITE WORKS:

HIS/HER FAVORITE STUFF:

DATES:

HANGS WITH:

OTHER:

NAME:

BORN:

LIVES:

MY FAVORITE WORKS:

HIS/HER FAVORITE STUFF:

DATES:

HANGS WITH:

OTHER:

FIND heroes >>>>

AT *home.*

NAME:

BORN:

LIVES:

MY FAVORITE WORKS:

HIS/HER FAVORITE STUFF:

DATES:

HANGS WITH:

OTHER:

NAME:

BORN:

LIVES:

MY FAVORITE WORKS:

HIS/HER FAVORITE STUFF:

DATES:

HANGS WITH:

OTHER:

NAME:

BORN:

LIVES:

MY FAVORITE WORKS:

HIS/HER FAVORITE STUFF:

DATES:

HANGS WITH:

OTHER:

NAME:

BORN:

LIVES:

MY FAVORITE WORKS:

HIS/HER FAVORITE STUFF:

DATES:

HANGS WITH:

OTHER:

IT IS
BETTER

TO LIVE RICH THAN TO DIE RICH. —SAMUEL JOHNSON

NAME:

BORN:

LIVES:

MY FAVORITE WORKS:

HIS/HER FAVORITE STUFF:

DATES:

HANGS WITH:

OTHER:

Stars

NAME:

BORN:

LIVES:

MY FAVORITE WORKS:

HIS/HER FAVORITE STUFF:

DATES:

HANGS WITH:

OTHER:

NAME:

BORN:

LIVES:

MY FAVORITE WORKS:

HIS/HER FAVORITE STUFF:

DATES:

HANGS WITH:

OTHER:

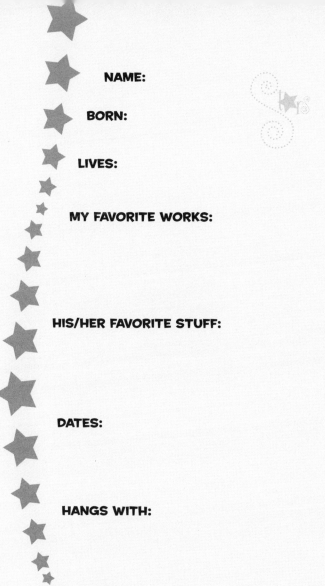

NAME:

BORN:

LIVES:

MY FAVORITE WORKS:

HIS/HER FAVORITE STUFF:

DATES:

HANGS WITH:

OTHER:

WE ARE
ALL IN
THE
GUTTER . . . .

BUT
SOME
OF US
ARE
LOOKING
AT
THE
STARS.
—OSCAR WILDE

DIARY
A SPECIAL PLACE FOR YOUR EVERYDAY THOUGHTS.

DREAM JOURNAL
CATCH THEM. KEEP THEM. LIVE THEM.

SOCIAL JOURNAL
GOSSIP, FRIENDS, ADDRESSES, HOT SPOTS.

SOUL JOURNAL
AFFIRM, EXPLORE, RECORD YOUR TRUTH.

BLANK JOURNAL
THERE'S NOTHING BLANK ABOUT YOU.

COLLECT THEM ALL!

KILLER COPY BY JEFF MUELLER AT FLOATING HEAD.
FUNKY DESIGN BY JENNIFER GORDON @ VELVETELVIS.COM
RETRO TYPE BY FONT DINER AND HOUSE INDUSTRIES.